Concise Guide to Self-Publishing
You Can Do It!
What You Need To Know

Mike Miller

Copyright © 2020 Mike Miller.

Cover clip art from www.clker.com, used with permission.

You may contact the author at pubyourbook@gmail.com.

ISBN: 9798650697688

Printed in the United States of America.

Table of Contents

First Things First	1
About This Booklet	1
The More You Know	1
What is Self-Publishing?	2
Other Books on Self-Publishing	3
Resource Links	4
A Disclaimer	4
Managing Your Book Project	5
Why? => Motivation	5
Quality – It's Your Responsibility	5
Planning	5
S.M.A.R.T. Planning	6
Detours	6
Market Research	7
Your Customer's and Customers' Heads	7
A Book? Me? Write A Book?	7
Your Audience(s) = Your Market(s)	8
Value	8
Feelings	9
"I already wrote my book"	9
Revenues, Royalties, Costs	9
Pricing	9
Content – Words & Images	10
Self-Defense	10
Breaking the Creativity Block	10
"Write what you know."	11
Transferring Thought to Manuscript	11
Read, wRite, Review, Revise	12
Critiquing	12
Critiquing Apps	13
Guidelines for Critiquing	13
ReVision	14
Keeping Track of Details	14
Word Processor Features Make Writing Easier	15
Some Common Writing Errors	17
Principles of Punctuation	17
Images	18

Formatting Fun	19
Physical Book Characteristics	19
Cover	20
Color Interior?	21
"Typical" Book Organization	21
Images	23
Formatting for Kindle	23
Self-Publishing and KDP	24
KDP Royalties	24
KDP.Amazon.com Book Process	25
Paperback Details	25
Paperback Content	26
Upload Manuscript	26
Launch Previewer	26
Ordering Proof Copy	28
Paperback Rights & Pricing	29
Marketing/Selling on Amazon.com	30
Kindlepreneur	30
Kindle Select	30
Kindle Unlimited and Kindle Owners Lending Library	30
Kindle Countdown Deals	31
Kindle Pricing	31
Selling = Getting Out There	32
Getting Your Book into Your Reader's Hands	32
Objections	35
Other Publishing Approaches	36
Fulfillment	37
Hybrid	37
Middleman	38
"They Want MY Book"	38
Profitability	38
SPS Contract	39
Copyright	40
Use Rights	40
Financial	42
About the Author	44
Acknowledgements	45
Your Project Profile	46

First Things First

About This Booklet

This guide covers a lot of material, perhaps more than a beginning author wants to deal with. Depending on your experience level, your goals, your ambitions, your schedule, your whatever, you may choose to ignore or delay some of the advice and processes I mention here. I suggest you read this complete booklet once to decide what applies to your book project. I've tried to keep this book short and compact, yet cover all the relevant self-publishing points.

I've worked with first-time authors who have put together a teaser book to evaluate the trade-off between creativity/writing, and self-publishing. Their motivation was to learn enough about the self-publishing process to enable them to make deliberate decisions about what tasks they want to do themselves, and what tasks they want to outsource for their first "real" book. Many of these authors discovered that they could take on most of or all of their book projects themselves. I encourage all authors and wannabees whom I talk with, to ask questions. In that process they get some answers and clarifications, and I gain more insight into how to educate and guide them.

The More You Know

The more you know, the higher the probability of your success in your book project. This may seem obvious, but frequently a writer may feel overwhelmed with "so many things to consider". Better to realize the magnitude and stages of the project early on and make decisions that can help prevent downstream problems, delays, and frustrations. Here I focus on what you need to know/do to create and publish your book. I have a companion book (*It's Your Book...*), available on Amazon.com, going into much more detail.

Your book-writing project will depend on technology: computer (PC or MAC), tablet (Android or Apple), or phone (Android or Apple) apps, the cloud, and more. These evolve, offering new features and changes. I've purposely stayed away from most technical discussion, except for certain word processing features that can significantly ease the writing and formatting process.

What is Self-Publishing?

Self-publishing is a strategy to make your book available to a market without your having to go through the delaying steps of soliciting and signing an agent and/or a "traditional" publisher.

There are two main players in the self-publishing: print-on-demand (POD) services and self-publishing services (SPS). The distinguishing characteristic is how much of the whole publishing process they address. The POD organizations focus on satisfying purchases of published books. KDP and Ingram are the two largest POD services. The SPS organizations offer a broad array of fee-based services for the self-published (aka indie) author.

POD is a digital technology that removes the need for inventorying books. SPSs offer a broad array of services to support authors throughout much of the writing, formatting, publishing, and distribution process. One of the services they offer either directly or indirectly is a print-on-demand (POD) service.

KDP (Kindle Direct Publishing) is an Amazon company offering POD services. They do not offer the services offered by the self-publishing services. SPS may use KDP, they may use other print-on-demand services, or they may operate their own print-on-demand service.

Some say self-publishing is "doing all the work yourself". Not exactly. Many services can help in the "self-publishing" process. These services can include marketing, several types of editing, content design, layout, cover design, collateral creation, online sales, printing, distribution, publicity, and more. Taking advantage of these services may allow you more opportunity to focus on your creativity. But you must establish your self-publishing goals and identify viable helpers along the way. These steps include assessing yourself, and assessing and evaluating potential SPS candidates, selecting and negotiating a work plan, and marketing/selling your book. There is a lot to deal with. Compared to traditional publishing, self-publishing can dramatically accelerate the process of getting your book "out there", and can result in higher per-book revenues.

The more of your book project you are comfortable doing yourself and have the opportunity to do, the lower your costs will be, the sooner your book will achieve break-even and start earning profit for you. The last chapter in this book is a checklist of the major items for you to consider as you evaluate your project: what you can do yourself, what you need to learn more about, and what you may want to engage others to help.

I've read and heard comments that using "self-publishing services" means that you are not really self-publishing. I don't buy that notion, although it is important to verify that you own the copyrights and all rights to your book.

There are many books addressing various aspects of the book business: writing, self-publishing, marketing, selling, creating email lists, etc. This booklet takes a different approach. My goal is to help you become more knowledgeable on the overall book process so you can develop a clear direction to the completion of your book. Many SPSs assume that you already have your book content ready to market and sell. Maybe you do, maybe you don't, or it's not done, or it's stuck in your head, or you don't know what to do next in your book project/business. That's a reason for this booklet. Your book, your book project, is a business; it has outgoes and incomes for you to manage.

I'm partial to and focus on **KDP** (kdp.amazon.com/) (Kindle Direct Publishing), **Microsoft Word** (www.microsoft.com/), The **GIMP** image editor (www.gimp.org/). There are self-publishing services other than KDP, other word processing apps (Libre Office (www.libreoffice.org/), Google Docs (www.google.com/), WordPerfect (www.wordperfect.com/), Apple Pages (www.apple.com/), and several image processing apps (Adobe Photoshop (www.adobe.com/), paint.net (www.getpaint.net/), etc.). Online clipart sources include free clker (www.clker.com/), and reasonably priced GoGraph.com (www.gograph.com/). There are alternatives for all these apps.

Other Books on Self-Publishing

If you search Amazon.com for 'self publishing' you will get over 90,000 hits, most with a narrow focus, selling, marketing, writing, social media, more. As your book project proceeds, you may want to look at some of those books; many are available as low-cost Kindle books, with immediate access.

You can search Amazon using keywords relevant to what information you need. Then click on a possible book, and use *Look Inside* to see if it addresses your needs. That's the approach some of your customers will use to locate your book(s).

Resource Links

I have provided links to online resources. These links are not exhaustive – there are many relevant resources online and in print. The self-publishing world is evolving. I have not included links to any PODs other than KDP. If you are reading this on a Kindle or in a Kindle app, you may click on the link.

A Disclaimer

I use KDP for my own books and for the books I design for my clients. I receive nothing for endorsing the KDP print on demand service.

Managing Your Book Project

Why? => Motivation

Why do you want to write a book? Share what you know? Earn some money? Leave a legacy? And many other reasons.

Motivation is vital to your book project. At times, you may wonder whether your creative effort is worth the energy that it consumes. And if you have a team (whether one or several people) supporting you, their interest or commitment may wane. This is why answering "Why?" and revisiting "Why?" as your project proceeds is important.

Quality – It's Your Responsibility

The quality of your book is your responsibility. Here is where due diligence is important. Quality of your content (text & images), layout, cover design, color selection, image clarity, grammar, punctuation, marketing materials, interviews, etc. You can delegate tasks to others, but responsibility for the quality of your book remains with you. You make all the decisions. Your book is your expression of your vision. After all, *It's Your Book*.

Planning

We've all heard of Plan A. But it's really Plan B, Plan C, etc., that deliver the finished product. Your plans include tasks, responsibilities, schedule, costs: your own and those of your team. Your readers are on your team. Two important questions in planning are "What's next?" and "What can go wrong?"

The best way to create your plan is to start at the end, for example, the date you want your book to be available on Amazon.com. Then work back from there. Starting at the end is a big step toward staying focused. As you work back you may discover that your hoped-for availability date is not reasonable. This is an important bit of information that you need to realize early in your process. What to do about it? Find other ways to complete on your hoped-for schedule. Or change your target date.

S.M.A.R.T. Planning

SMART is an acronym commonly used in planning. Goals must be:

Specific – what needs to be completed at each step.

Manageable – and can be managed to be completed.

Appropriate – to deliver what's needed.

Realistic – and be realistic and important for your project.

Timely – and be completed when necessary.

Detours

Detours can occur anywhere in your book project.

Detours test your knowledge, your resilience, your flexibility, your transparency, your openness.

Planning helps anticipate and manage detours.

Market Research

Your Customer's and Customers' Heads

That section heading looks odd, but maybe it's memorable. You need to know what your customers (individuals and groups) need and want and then how to make them aware that you can satisfy their needs and wants. Here are some thought-prompts about your readers:

Their needs – the must haves or your book is a no-go for them.

Their wants – not a must have, but they really would like it.

Their expectations – what they expect to gain from your book.

Their options – what else can they satisfy their needs?

And, how your book will:

Satisfy their needs and wants;

Provide the value they seek.

A Book? Me? Write A Book?

Sure! You have ideas, experiences, insights, inspirations, memories that you want to share with *others*. Who are these *others*?

The *others* are your audience(s), your market(s), those who may be interested in your book, may buy your book, may read your book.

"I have nothing new to say, nothing new to offer." Not true. If that's what you believe, stop, take a step back, and challenge yourself to establish your uniqueness.

Uniqueness? Yes, we are all different. We share limited experiences and knowledge with others. Everyone is *unique*. This may trite, but it's true. Once you start thinking of yourself as unique, you start to realize how unique you are. And, as a corollary, what unique value you can offer to your readers.

Your Audience(s) = Your Market(s)

Your audiences are the collections of readers interested in what you have to say. They might want to know more about how to do something, more about something they are interested in (and you are interested in). They may want to be entertained, to be educated, to be challenged, etc. They may want to know more about you, about your writing.

To identify your market, answer these questions about your hoped-for readers: Who are they? Where are they? How will you reach them? Why will they read your book? Why will they buy your book? How much will they pay for your book? What are their expectations for your book? How will they value your book? What options do they have? Answer these questions early in your book-writing endeavor so that what you write satisfies those needs and wants, and is marketable and saleable.

Satisfying needs and wants is a major step in establishing a relationship with your readers. Why a relationship? The relationship demonstrates mutual respect, you for your readers, your readers for you.

Value

Answers to the why, who, what, where, when, how questions help determine your book's VALUE to your audience, guiding your writing process and your pricing – all aspects of your book project/business.

"What if my book is free?" It's not free. Your "free" book has an opportunity cost for your readers. Your reader should want to *invest* time in reading your book, not just *spend* time.

Your audience has options to satisfy its needs and wants: other books, YouTube videos, online and onsite classes, and even doing nothing. Don't underestimate that last option.

People don't buy things. They buy value. How to solve a problem, seize an opportunity, gain insight, develop feelings. Make sure your book provides the value they seek. Value is a major influence on setting price.

Feelings

Your audience wants to come away from the experience of reading your book with better than just "positive" feelings. Feelings feed word-of-mouth in your book process.

"I already wrote my book"

Isn't it too late for this needs and wants stuff?

You likely did some sort of informal needs and wants considerations before you started writing. So, you have an idea for who your market is. I suggest you formalize, aka write down, your informal knowledge of your audience.

You may feel that your market definition is constrained by what you've already written. That's an assumption, challenge it. Identify your market independent of what you've already written. You always have the option of revising your book, and such revisions may be minor tweaks. In any event, identifying your market will help your revision phase and your selling phase. Your analysis may provide fodder for a later book.

Revenues, Royalties, Costs

There are several ways your book can generate revenue: royalties from online sales, profit from self-sell, sales in brick and mortar stores, bundled into a another offering, a class, a workshop, a lecture series, a discussion panel. The two components of revenue are royalties and costs, covered later in the **Self-Publishing and KDP** and the **Other Publishing Approaches** chapters.

Pricing

Key to revenue calculation are the retail price for your book and the printing costs. Pricing strategies include: value pricing, pricing based on the market pricing of competitive and complementary books or services, and pricing based on number of pages.

Content – Words & Images

Self-Defense

Before you get into the creation of your book, you need to set up a process to protect your work from loss due to equipment failure, editing mistakes, viruses, and other "attacks". Can you wait until you have much of your manuscript written before doing this? Yes, BUT I recommend against waiting – do it in the beginning, and be disciplined in creating backups.

Save your manuscript frequently, and copy it to the cloud or to another drive as a backup. I'm obsessive about this, I may save a manuscript every 20 minutes. I use Total Commander (www.ghisler.com/) ZIP file creator to help manage files and folders. It is inexpensive and easy to use. On Windows, you can use File Explorer | Send To | Compressed (zip) folder. Either way, rename the file extension (.zip) to a sequential number, starting with .000, and incrementing for each step for version tracking. This strategy allows me to revert to previous versions or to recover text from previous versions.

Breaking the Creativity Block

"But I don't know how to write." "But I can't get started." "I can't . . ."

These are opinions, not facts.

What is your genre? Fiction? Nonfiction? Poetry? How-to? Each of these has several sub-genres (science fiction, romance, etc.). Unsure? Pick one now, let your genre selection evolve.

> Whether you think you can
> or think you can't,
> you're right.
> ~Henry Ford

There are several paths to starting and to continuing your book project: join a writing group, take writing classes, read a lot, just start writing about anything.

I often hear "I have a story to tell, but I don't know how to do it". Or friends tell you "you could/should write a book" on your experiences.

My advice: just get started: write a short story, an anecdote, a poem, a list, anything. Whatever you choose to write need not be in your genre. The goal is to activate the writing-portion of your brain. Writing prompts are everywhere, newspaper articles, websites, blogs, advertisements.

Anything? You will find your writing draws you in certain directions, you will soon find some interests worth pursuing. Some writers can sit down and write. Some let their subconscious chew on a topic for some time, then sit down and write.

Some writer-wannabees don't write because they feel their first attempt won't be good, or won't be good enough. My advice: Get over it. Don't self-sabotage. The writing process is a Read – wRite – Review – Revise cycle.

Sit in front of your keyboard, grab a pad and pen, talk to your tablet's or phone's speech-to-text app.

"Write what you know."

That's what "they" say. (Who are "they" anyway?) Sure, but do some research, learn more, expand your content knowledge, your market knowledge, and your writing knowledge. Take writing or journalism classes in local community colleges or online. Check out TED (**T**echnology, **E**ntertainment, **D**esign) (www.ted.com/); Udemy (www.udemy.com/); The Great Courses (www.thegreatcourses.com/). Google MOOC (Massive Online Open Course).

Transferring Thought to Manuscript

Typing, scanning, downloading, and copy-paste are all viable methods for collecting the text content for your book. Technology on Android and Apple tablets and phones has advanced to the point where **Speech-to-Text** apps do a respectable job of converting your spoken word into editable text. Suggestions for improving the quality of the dictation: speak clearly, at a normal speaking rate, minimize background noise. After you've dictated the text, review it for homophones (different words that sound alike), wrong words, incorrect punctuation, strange autocorrects, and other errors. Some apps may require internet access; some have a speech-training requirement; some may have limited language support.

Read, wRite, Review, Revise

The four 'R's of writing. ☺

Read a lot. I've heard some writers say that they are concerned about mimicking what others have written. The more you read, the less likely that is to happen. When I read, I note word usage. Why was this word used? Why didn't the author use another word? Challenging word usage can be a mind-expanding experience.

Writing groups, some call them writers' groups can help. They are congenial groups, all members have the opportunity to contribute, to challenge, and to help members to succeed. Ask at local libraries or bookstores about writing groups.

Seek advice at a writers' group meeting. Offer to show some of your writing at the meeting. Ask for member's comments. Check out (www.6ftferrets.com/).

"But I have nothing to offer the group."

Not true, and you will realize that after attending a couple of meetings. Member's and members' comments are vital to growth. Critiques and critiquers help writers become authors.

Gather your ideas and thoughts. Write them down, as rough or as polished as you wish. Set them aside for a few days. Then review and refine.

"Is that how professional writers work?" Yes. The best writers go through this write, review, revise cycle. Several times.

Critiquing

The goal of critiquing is quality improvement. Critiquing is an essential part of the review/revise process. Note, that's **critique** not **criticize**.

In the critiquing process, a writer provides content (for example, a few pages, maybe 1000 words) for the group to read and discuss. My preference, and the most productive, is for the author to provide printed copy or emailed copy for the members to read before or at a meeting, or for take-home critiquing. The author, another member, or a computer voice, may read the manuscript aloud. Another member or computer voice reader can be beneficial since the author's emphasis will be missing; the words and their nuances, emotion, and symbolism must stand-alone. Another choice is silent read from the printed manuscript, like happens in a library, bookstore, or online where the author is not present.

Offering a critique at a meeting after several minutes of reading, rereading, and/or thinking is limited, and could be a disservice to the author and the critiquers. At-home critiques allow the critiquer to do a more thorough job.

Don't depend on friends or family members to do a solid critique of your writing. Some might, but some might not be objective. They won't want to hurt your feelings. You want to enlist the aid of what Stephen King calls his "Ideal Reader", his *IR*, someone, friend, family, other, who will do serious critiquing.

There are several apps for "critiquing" writing. These apps provide a level of copyediting (spelling, grammar, punctuation, word selection) but do not provide the content evaluation only a human reader can provide. Despite that limitation, they are valuable for analysis of your writing. Google: 'grammar checking tools' for a list.

Critiquing Apps

I find MS Word spelling and grammar checker to be useful. There are a number of online critiquing apps, some fee based, some free: (Autocrit (www.autocrit.com/), Grammarly (app.grammarly.com/), ProWritingAid (prowritingaid.com/), Wordrake (www.wordrake.com/), and others). They are useful for analyzing visible characteristics of your manuscript, but they do not analyze content, meaning, nuance, emotion, etc.

Guidelines for Critiquing

Always be positive and be specific ("I like that story" or "Good job" are far too vague, and don't help the author or the critiquing process). Critiques are suggestions, and you need not accept any suggestions. No one should be offended. As a corollary, if you are offended, then maybe you are not cut out to be an author.

Critiquers should identify and point out areas that may need attention and describe the concern. Critiquers do not rewrite what you wrote – it's your work. Consider why certain words were used or not used. Authors and critiquers should listen to the critiques. You, as the author, should not respond to critiques other than to thank the critiquer. When the critiquing of your writing is complete, you MAY say something about the work. It's IMPORTANT that your writing stands on its own. If you feel you need to defend something that you wrote, maybe what you wrote needs clarification.

ReVision

Some types of revision are simple, spelling, punctuation, word choice, narrative flow. As you write your book, you have a Vision (formal or informal) for the trajectory of the chapters and for the book. The trajectory may include the desired conclusion or points to be covered. Maybe the critique raises some concerns such that you might need to ReVisit the writing. This may be easy to do – hurray! This may be difficult to do – that's OK. Maybe the trajectory is weak. Maybe it doesn't flow well. There are a number of reasons for ReVision.

Don't give up – it's better to cycle through the ReVision phase(s) before you've published your book. Unpublishing a book is possible, but it wastes your time, may cost you money, and may result in lost readership.

I purchased one book where a ReVision cycle could have transformed a semi-adequate book into a strong book. A waste of my time, my money, and certainly one lost customer for that author.

Keeping Track of Details

Keeping track of details is vital to the quality of your writing. Let's call the mechanism you use for this purpose a *catalog of details*. Your catalog need not use technology, but there are apps that can help. Some details to include: character names (consistent spelling), ethnicity, heritage, family, relationships, relevant dates (birth, graduation, marriage, death, etc.), travel, education, job/career, financial situation, preferred clothing, and more. This is information builds the realities of your character's and characters' demographics. The same considerations apply to locations, buildings, travel, vehicles, etc. - their demographics. My rule-of-thumb is that each time I reference a character or a location I verify/update the reference to be properly documented in my catalog, and update the catalog as my characters and locations evolve.

There are a number of ways to manage your content and keep track of details: outlining, storyboarding, flash cards, using PowerPoint, the *Snowflake* method (www.advancedfictionwriting.com/). The snowflake method is a discipline to help you consistently reference character, location, and any other relevant information in your book(s).

The catalog of details is useful in any book series that keeps characters in several books.

Word Processor Features Make Writing Easier

I find that establishing the page layout parameters early and editing the manuscript using those parameters helps in my overall book layout process. You may choose to do this or to use a default format and change it later. As I created this booklet, I set the page size to 6"x9", with appropriate margins, the format of the intended deliverable print book.

Allow the word processor to handle line endings based on your margins. Don't use spans of spaces or tabs or [Enter]s for formatting. Their use can make tuning the format tedious. This becomes obvious and frustrating when you change the page size or margin sizes.

To advance to the next paragraph, press [Enter]. (next verse in poetry)

To advance to the next page, press [Ctrl][Enter].

In poetry you may need to advance to the next line in a verse: press [Shift][Enter].

To force two words to remain adjacent at end-of-line use [Ctrl][Shift][Space] instead of [Space] between the words. This is known as a keep-space. For example, if your writing includes a date at the end of a line, July 4, for example, you do not want the date to be split over two lines – that just doesn't look right. A keep-space between July and 4 solves that problem.

Two ways to handle indents: set a style (preferred) or use tabs. Styles are used to manage font, font size, font characteristics, indentation, line spacing, and paragraph spacing. Styles simplify tuning a document format. For example, the style *Normal* applies to the paragraphs in a chapter. If I want to change the font in all the "normal" paragraphs, I modify the font selection for that *Normal*. When I click OK the font changes for all the *Normal* paragraphs.

You can make your own styles. For my book design projects, I have formatting styles for poetry, fiction, nonfiction, stars (the * * * paragraph separators), images, tables, and more. The styles simplify the content layout process.

On the menu bar, Page Layout provides controls for detailed page layout and page breaks. These are valuable features and are worth your time learning how to use them.

If the formatting changes you are trying to make don't seem to be working, "there's a button for that". The pilcrow (¶) button on the word processor ribbon is a toggle to show what's really in the document (the hidden characters).

I generally leave the pilcrow toggle on so hidden characters are visible when I'm typing or editing and I always know what I'm working with. Seeing the hidden characters on the screen can be distracting for some writers.

Always leave word processor **spell check** and **grammar check** features enabled. You don't have to honor the suggestions but they might help with some finer grammar points.

You can create an automatic **Table of Contents** (ToC), useful in some nonfiction, using the paragraph heading styles. Here's how: insert page numbers, bottom center of each page. Place the cursor where you want the ToC to occur in your manuscript. On the WP ribbon: [References] [Table of Contents] [Automatic Table 1]. Refining the ToC can be done later in your book project. To update the ToC after document editing, place the cursor in it, [Right-Click][Update Field]. If given a choice, select *Update All* rather than *Update Page Numbers Only*.

There are many more tips and tricks to aid in creating/tuning the final version of your book: columns, tables, headers, footers, etc. These are far more detailed than I address in this booklet. The word processor help-text or a YouTube video may provide enough information for you to explore these features. When you figure out how to use any of the more complicated features document your procedure. This will save you a lot of time and frustration later.

If you are experimenting with or learning about styles, I suggest you create an experimental version of your manuscript, named as such, solely for that experimentation, so that your real manuscript doesn't get messed up if something goes wrong.

Some Common Writing Errors

Tense shifting. If your book/story takes place in one timeframe then you want to avoid or at least minimize changing verb tense. Some books, some genres require multiple tenses. For example, a historical narrative (what happened - *past*) with explanatory narrative (what it means - *present*).

Point of View (PoV) shifting. There are four points of view: first person (I, we), second person (you), third person (he, she, they), and omniscient – a variety of third person (the narrator knows all or the narrator has limited knowledge). PoV shifting can be useful is it's done deliberately.

Subject/object usage. ('between you and me', not 'between you and I').

Subject/verb agreement (usually singular/plural conflicts).

Passive voice is generally thought to be weak ☺, but there are places where it is useful.

When in doubt, check the context. (The context is what happens before, during, and after the current moment.)

Verify that the dialog/dialect are realistic and appropriate for the emotion, location, and action.

Challenge each word. Why that word? Why not another word? This may sound tedious, but this accomplishes two things: improved word selection during the revision process and improved word selection in a later writing process.

Principles of Punctuation

Proper punctuation is a tool for clarity and for confusion avoidance. There are several grammar standards guides; the two I reference are the Chicago Manual of Style and the Associated Press Style Guide. These standards make different recommendations for certain situations. I am a fan of the Oxford comma (aka Harvard comma or serial comma): the comma used between the second-to-last element on a list and the "and"/"or" conjunction, unless the second-to-last element and the last element are considered a single item.

Sentence or phrase ending punctuation errors can easily occur. The typical sentence/phrase ending characters are these: **. , : ; ? !)] }**. The error is that one or more "white space" characters (space or tab) precedes any of these characters. Depending on your genre and writing style there may be other sentence ending characters. Use your word processor **Find** or **Find and Replace** command to locate these and correct them.

The placement of the period or comma inside or outside a quoted text area (single or double quotation mark) often causes debate. An easy way to pick the correct placement is to treat the period like the exclamation mark or the question mark: where would they appear relative to the quotation mark? That's where the period or comma goes.

Images

Images are important in many books. The first place an image matters is the front cover, and color can be an attention attracter. An image on the back cover is valuable; it could be your picture, helping to establish a relationship with you. If your book's spine is wide enough, you may consider an image there. I suggest color images for the cover – there is no extra cost for a color cover using KDP.

Depending on your genre, you may want to include images – artwork and technical or engineering explanatory images. Color interior images can triple (approximately) the cost of your book, even if there is only one color pixel.

There are several free or low cost online clipart or photography sources (I use and recommend clker.com, gograph.com). Always check the copyright permission requirements.

Formatting Fun

Formatting is fun because it tunes the appearance of your book to what you want your reader to see and feel. In MS Word **styles** are a powerful formatting tool.

Physical Book Characteristics

Book dimensions (for example, 6"x9", but there are other sizes) defines/affects other characteristics. The number of pages, the font and font size, and the type/thickness of the paper determine the spine width.

Page layout deals with the appearance of the content (text and images) on the printed page. Setting the margins (top, bottom, left, right, and gutter) establishes the printable/nonprintable areas. The gutter is the spine-area within the book – important to ensure text doesn't creep into that area. Too narrow a gutter is unprofessional, makes the book less comfortable to open/read, and can damage the spine. When the margins are determined, the headers and footers, including page numbering can be set up.

The first page of each chapter may have special formatting requirements, such as chapter heading drop down, font and font size, text characteristics. Chapter headings and subheadings can be used to create an optional automatic Table of Contents.

Paragraph characteristics include justification (left-justified, right-ragged (as in the print version of this book); right-justified, left-ragged (seldom used); centered (a specialty format); left/right justified (typical in many books). I have read anecdotal (nonscientific) evidence that left-justified right-ragged is easier to read than left/right justified.

There are two typical methods of paragraph separation. In fiction, indent the first line of each paragraph. In nonfiction, use a blank line between paragraphs.

Font and font size affect the readability of the text. Text can be serif (little ticks on the letters, like Times New Roman in this book) or non-serif (Arial is an example). Anecdotally, serif fonts are easier to read. Large-print books (for the visually impaired) use large font sizes (for example, 18 point), increasing the number of pages in your book, and making your book available to a larger audience. You might consider publishing two versions of your book, one with a regular font size, and one large print. This requires an ISBN for each book.

Simple page numbering starts with a number on the title page, incrementing to the last page. This look amateurish. Traditional page numbering can be more involved to set up, using
Page Layout | Breaks | Next Page, and not showing page number on early pages in your book (see **"Typical" Book Organization** below.)

Cover

The book dimensions determine the cover size. Things to consider on the cover include images (or not), color, bleed (images extend to the edge), Your book in a bookstore will be displayed in one of two ways: front-visible or spine-visible. In both cases you will want to use color to attract attention.

When the cover of your book is displayed online, its display size will be 1" wide. Make sure the title and subtitle are large enough at 1" width to be readable.

The ISBN block appears on the back cover, lower right side. When you design the back cover, keep that placement in mind so it does not cover anything important. I suggest that you not include price on the block or on the book cover.

The front-spine edge and the back-spine edge transition can be problematic if your book has a color change. The issue is the variation in the printing equipment.

The back cover blurb should describe enough of your book for a book-browser to read and assess your book's value to them. You may want to include "About the Author" information to establish some credibility.

ISBN = International Standard Book Number

KDP can provide a free ISBN number; the listing on Amazon will show "Independently Published". You can buy your own ISBN from Bowker.com. KDP authors can buy an ISBN at a discounted rate from Bowker. If you use your own ISBN, the listing on Amazon.com will show a publisher name that you specify. Reference Bowker.com (www.bowker.com/) for more information. Having an ISBN number is essential to be listed in Books In Print, necessary for retail sale in bookstores and placement in libraries.

Color Interior?

Some books may benefit from or require color interior. Printing books with a color interior, can result in a significant increase of printing cost (a factor of 3 or more).

"Typical" Book Organization

The following organization is typical; many authors put some items (for example, Acknowledgments) in different locations in their book.

Contents	Notes
"End Papers"	Blank pages at the very beginning and end of your manuscript. These pages can be used for note-taking and/or to increase the number of pages to widen the spine supporting a more readable printed text on the spine.
"Front Matter" starts	A convenient characterization of the following section of the book.
Title page	Highly suggested.
Copyright Page	Highly suggested.
Disclaimers, attributions	Suggested.
Dedication	Suggested.
Table of Contents	Optional, usually in nonfiction, anthologies, page numbers start with 'i', MS Word automated generation.
Table of Illustrations	Optional, usually nonfiction, MS Word automated generation.
Epigraph	Optional, a book-relevant quotation.
Foreword	Optional, written by other than the author.
Preface	Optional, information about the book topic but not part of the book itself.
"Front Matter" ends	Page numbers start with '1'.

Contents	Notes
Introduction	Suggested, overview of the book, could be marketing oriented. Readers often skip reading the Introduction.
Prologue	Optional, background information or backstory.
Body	Required, chapters, subchapters, footnotes (optional), images, tables.
"Back Matter" starts	A convenient characterization of the following section of the book.
End Notes	Optional, "footnotes".
References	Optional material used in preparing content, and other references for readers.
Epilog	Optional chapter to bring closure to the book, can describe the fates of the characters, and can hint at a sequel.
Afterword	An optional Afterword may describe observations made during the writing of the book, speaking to the reader.
Appendix (appendices)	Optional, listing recommended books, websites, organizations, worksheets, or other resources. Citation formatting standards.
Glossary	Optional, lists words and their definitions, sometimes placed at the front of the book.
Bibliography	Optional, lists references in book, and may include other books of potential interest to the reader.
Index	Optional, usually nonfiction books, alphabetical order. MS Word provides an Index generation feature.
Acknowledgments	Optional, acknowledge support of others, individuals and groups, may be placed at front of book.
About the Author	Suggested, a relationship builder.
"Back Matter" ends	Could be some blank pages.

Images

>Resolution at least 200 dpi, 300 dpi preferred.
>RGB color works, need not be CMYK.
>Always submit images in color, POD can convert to grayscale.
>Can be photos, scans, internet downloads.

Formatting for Kindle

Formatting eBooks differs from formatting print books. eBooks don't use page numbers, page headings, or page footings. The font size is reader selectable. The Table of Contents in an eBook uses internal links rather than page numbers.

Some eBook readers allow reader annotation. The annotations may be printable or email-able.

Free Kindle reader apps are available for PCs and MACs, and an eBook downloaded to a Kindle device is available on others free (using same account name), synced for reading.

Some readers may purchase an eBook and read through it – then. if the book merits being written in (!), the reader may purchase a printed copy. I'm one of those readers.

Sometimes post-publication updates to an eBook are distributed free to those who downloaded it. This is a valuable feature.

Self-Publishing and KDP

I'm partial to Amazon and Kindle Direct Publishing (KDP). If you are unsure about using KDP for your own book, the **Other Publishing Approaches** chapter, later, explores other publishing options.

There are many self-publishing services offering to help you self-publish your book. For a fee. I've explored several of these for my own writings and on behalf of my clients. I keep coming back to KDP, Kindle Direct Publishing, an Amazon company.

The cost to self-publish with KDP could be as low as $0.00 if you do all the work yourself. I STRONGLY suggest purchasing and reviewing one printed proof copy. KDP offers a list of independent service providers for cover design, copyediting, etc. and KDP offers a cover creator app.

KDP provides exceptional support; the quality of their print product is excellent, their online submission procedure is straight forward, and their pricing is among the best.

The online KDP Help Center answers many questions about their KDP Self-Publishing process. (kdp.amazon.com/en_US/help)

KDP Royalties

Royalties are a function of printing cost and list price.

Printing cost - proof and self-sell copy cost chart.

Paperback Specifications	Page count	US Fixed Cost per book	Additional cost per page
Grayscale	24-108	$2.15	None
Grayscale	110-828	$0.85	$0.012
Color	24-40	$3.65	None
Color	42-500	$0.85	$0.07

The above chart taken from (www.authorimprints.com/amazon-kdp-royalty-pricing/)

KDP royalty calculation example:

(list price x 60%) - printing cost = royalty

For a 132 page grayscale book listed for $10:
Printing cost = $0.85 + 132 x $0.012 = $2.43.
Royalty = ($10 x 60%) − $2.43 = $6.00 - $2.43 = $3.57.

KDP.Amazon.com Book Process

Technology evolves. The process summary below is accurate as of the writing of this chapter. The KDP process consists of a number of steps/screens prompting you for information (aka metadata) about your book. Many of the prompts request obvious information. I've not listed those items but I've included explanations or hints about some of the information requested.

The first step is to create a KDP.Amazon.com account – name, address, email, banking information (for royalties), credit card information (for proof and self-sell copies). If you already have an Amazon.com account, you can use it.

The following sections represent the online screens in the KDP process.

Paperback Details

Language (what is the language of your book?)
Book Title
Subtitle (optional)
Series information (optional, if your book is part of a series)
Edition Number (optional)
Author Name, can be pseudonym
Contributors (optional): role and name
Description (4000 characters can be provided later)
Publishing Rights:
Select one: I own the copyright OR public domain work
Keywords (up to 7)
Categories (1 or 2) – suggest two different areas
[Save and Continue]

Paperback Content

Print ISBN: Select one: Free from KDP OR Use My Own
Publication Date (optional, you can set one, or when book goes live)
Print Options
  Interior & Paper Type:
  Select one: B&W on cream OR B&W on white OR Color on white
  Trim Size: 6"x9" or select a different size
  Bleed Settings
Select one: No Bleed or Bleed (pdf only)
  Paperback Cover Finish: Select one: Matte or Glossy

Upload Manuscript

[Upload paperback manuscript] (file type: .doc, .docx, .pdf, .rtf, .html) (Select file on your computer)
Wait for upload to complete...
Book Cover
Select one: Use cover Creator OR [Upload your cover file].
Upload a cover you already have (.pdf).

Note check box if you are providing your own ISBN number.
Book Preview.

After you have uploaded your manuscript and cover, note the **Summary** showing the physical description of your book and its printing cost.

What file type should you upload .doc, .docx or .pdf? Apps that convert .doc/.docx may operate differently. A .pdf file created by your word processor may look slightly different from the .pdf file created by KDP. If the .pdf file created by your word processor is problematic, try submitting the .doc/.docx to KDP. I have experienced one situation in which the word processor .pdf convertor did not handle a header format properly, but the KDP .pdf convertor handled it correctly.

I suggest including a file creation date/time in the filename, for example: concise_guide 0711 1545.docx, showing July 11 at 3:45pm.

Launch Previewer

When you press the [Launch Previewer] button, KDP formats your book. This may take several minutes. You will have the opportunity to preview your cover and book online, and to download the KDP-formatted version of your book. I recommend you download the formatted version and save it on the unlikely chance that your printed copy doesn't look like the on-screen preview of downloaded version.

At this point your book (cover and interior) are displayed and you can move through your book looking for any issues you may wish to address.

Some common issues include:
Text or images aren't within the interior or cover safe-area.
The gutter is too narrow for the number of pages, crowding the spine space.
General formatting issues, placement.
Overall look and feel.

Print Previewer, Title, [Download a PDF proof]
I strongly suggest saving the downloaded print preview file in case there are any issues appearing later when you order printed proof of author-sell copies.

Select one: [Back to Details] OR [Save as Draft] OR [Save and Continue].
(next step Pricing)

Verify the following:

Cover: noting the content relative to the safe-area marks.

Front: layout, color, positioning, font size, content is within safe area.

Back: content, images, positioning, room for ISBN, ISBN correct, all content is within safe area.

Spine printing: if any, wording, spelling, positioning, content is within safe area.

Cycle through all the content pages: title page through the last page.

The odd numbered pages are on the right side.

If each chapter starts on a right page, all such page numbers are odd.

The page numbers in the table of content are correct.

The chapter layout is correct.

The page headers and footers are correct.

Note the Verify list:
Title
Author
ISBN
Cover type
Binding type (Paperback)

Select one: [Exit Print Previewer] OR [Approve]

"Approve" on the previewer is approval to proceed to the next step in the publishing process. It is NOT for Approval for publication on Amazon.com. That approval happens in a later step.

The next step is the **Pricing** screen.

Ordering Proof Copy

On the Bookshelf, locate your book title.

Book title, click on the three dots to the right [• • •].

Order a printed proof copy (maximum 5)

Select Amazon market (probably Amazon.com)

Within 4 hours you will receive an email form Amazon to confirm your order and for you to select the shipped schedule.

As your book evolves, you may end up cycling through the submit/proof cycle more than once.

Review the printed proof. Look for any errors, clumsiness, things that might be better if different. Don't rush. Review the printed proof with red pen in hand. Mark every change boldly. After you have reviewed and marked up the proof copy, then make the changes in the book file, and resubmit.

Depending on the quantity and type of changes, you might want to get another printed proof.

Paperback Rights & Pricing

Here is where you specify the territories where you want your book to be sold, its selling the price, its primary marketplace, and whether you want Expanded Distribution.

In general, you want as broad a market as possible. One reason you might want to limit distribution is that the content may be offensive in certain areas.

When you select a price, note the royalty that each online full-price sale will generate.

The final action on this screen is Publish You Paperback Book.

Marketing/Selling on Amazon.com

Much of this section is lifted from or paraphrased from kdp.amazon.com.

Authorcentral.amazon (authorcentral.amazon.com/) is an important free tool, enabling your customers to learn more about you. You provide a biography, include a link to your blog/website (if you have one), and a list of your book(s). When a customer looks at your book on Amazon, a "Follow the Author" button appears. Clicking that button brings up the Author Central information, including links to each of your books. Even if you have just one book (so far), create your Author Central listing.

Kindlepreneur

Kindlepreneur (kindlepreneur.com/) is an independent marketing service that offers YouTube videos, and several workshops on marketing eBooks. Kindlepreneur is a very useful resource.

Kindle Select

Enrolling your eBook in **Kindle Select** program gives you the opportunity to reach more readers and earn more money. Enrolling in KDP Select makes your book eligible for 70% royalty earnings on sales to customers in Brazil, Japan, India, and Mexico.

Enrolling in Kindle Select also grants you access to a set of promotional tools. You can schedule a **Kindle Countdown Deal** for books available on Amazon.com and Amazon.co.uk or a Free Book Promotion (readers worldwide can get your book free for a limited time).

Kindle Unlimited and Kindle Owners Lending Library

Kindle Unlimited is a subscription program for readers that allows them to read as many books as they want. The Kindle Owners' Lending Library is a collection of books that Amazon Prime members who own a Kindle can choose one book from each month with no due dates. When you enroll in KDP Select, your books are automatically included in both programs. Your books will still be available for anyone to buy in the Kindle Store, and you'll continue to earn royalties from those sales. You can earn a share of the KDP Select Global Fund based on how many pages KU or KOLL customers read of your book.

Kindle Countdown Deals

Kindle Countdown Deals are a KDP Select benefit that lets authors, no matter where you're located, run limited-time discount promotions for your books that are available on Amazon.com and Amazon.co.uk. Customers will see both the regular price and the promotional price on the book's detail page, as well as a countdown clock showing how much time remains at the promotional price. You'll continue to earn your selected royalty rate on each sale during the promotion.

Kindle Pricing

KDP supports two royalty pricing schemes: 35% royalty or 70% royalty.

The rule is that eBooks priced "competitively", between $2.99 and $9.99 are eligible for the 70% royalty. Pricing above $9.99 will generate the 35% royalty.

There is a slight "delivery fee" based on the size of the eBook file at the 70% royalty level.

Several Websites suggest that $2.99 is a "sweet spot" price. At a lower price the purchaser may question the value of the book, and a higher price may cause a purchaser to skip over the book.

eBook pricing is easily changeable so you can experiment with pricing levels.

Selling = Getting Out There

Getting Your Book into Your Reader's Hands

Always **carry books, bookmarks, and business cards** along wherever you go. Conspicuously read your book while waiting in an office. Strike up a conversation with others waiting.

Whatever selling strategies and methods you use, track how well those methods work. You want to focus on those that generate high conversion rates, and tweak or abandon those that don't.

Book signings are important opportunities to build relationships and to secure sales. Attend as many as you can, as a seller, a buyer, or an observer. When you attend, request a list of attendees, and observe their display spaces, their customer interaction, their marketing collateral. Acknowledge that you are an author and ask questions. At many signings, I've seen authors sit behind their tables and wait for walk-ups. That doesn't build relationships. I stand in front of my table and engage readers in a conversation, asking what they like to read. If I have something to offer, I point that out. I point out other authors who have books in the reader's preferred genre.

If I sense the reader is uncomfortable with my presence, I back off immediately so they can finger my books. I usually provide a display copy for fingering.

In addition to your marketing collateral, you might offer a trinket, a pen, a snack, a bottle of water.

Price your books for an easy transaction. For example $10, tax included. There's no need to calculate sales tax and handle coins at a book signing.

Book groups may be a source for sales and leads, Some book groups sell copies of the next discussion book. Don't expect each member will buy a book, but this is a way to gain momentum.

Library talks are great opportunities – readers depend on libraries. Library members and card holders equate libararies with learning and entertainment.

Word of Mouth is free and can create momentum for your book sales. Word of mouth means the reader has been affected by your book, sees the value in your book, and relays the value experience in promoting your book.

Press releases and **articles** are excellent, free, targetable medium to getting your word out. They can be published in newspapers, magazines, industry and organization newsletters, on websites and blogs. Contact the publishers and request submission guidelines; some will allow photos. Some magazines have themed issues and plan a year ahead.

Advertising costs money, but is worth trying. I suggest using press releases first.

Classes and workshops can be great revenue generators depending on your genre. For example, for me a class on self-publishing brings in writers.

Promotions, like special one-time pricing or give-aways can motivate readers to purchase your book.

Elevator/barstool talk, aka the 20-second talk, is a good "ice-breaker". The purpose is not to sell your book, but to interest your audience, could be one person, to ask questions or listen to more about your book(s).

Social media, Facebook, Twitter, LinkedIn, Instagram, others are viable promotion avenues. You can use your personal account or you can create a business account. Advertising is available on business accounts. Try to get a broad "friend" base, and allow friends to share/post your content. This can be low cost way of getting out there.

Websites/blogs can help your marketing efforts. They can consume a lot of time, just like social media can. My suggestion is that you establish a discipline of limiting your website/blog interaction time and schedule.

You can include **videos** on websites or blogs, and on YouTube. These can be teasers to get attention and interest. Videos are especially useful if you have a service to sell in conjunction with your book.

Email provides a somewhat personal sense of communication, and distribution of email may be free (depending on volume). Creating a targeted email list can be done in several ways: email signup lists at signings, in classes, website/blog links, social media advertising. Expect that some email recipients will ask to be unsubscribed. [constantcontact (www.constantcontact.com/index.jsp), mailchimp (mailchimp.com/)]

Online reviews are available through Amazon (www.amazon.com), Goodreads (www.goodreads.com/)], Smashwords (www.smashwords.com/), Barnes & Noble (www.barnesandnoble.com/), and other organizations. Amazon categorizes reviews as "verified purchase" when the reviewer purchased the book through Amazon. Author self-sell books are not "verified purchase". Browsers may interpret reviews by verified purchasers as more important and independent than other reviews.

Special interest groups (aka SIGs) may provide a valuable audience.

Friends and Family are always a market, but this market may be limited.

Interviews - Newspapers, magazines, television (community, broadcast, and cable), radio, websites, social media can provide excellent interviewing opportunities. Provide a copy of your book and a list of important interview points, maybe questions for the interviewer to ask. Don't feel uncomfortable doing this – the interviewer and the interviewee want a win-win. The interviewer MAY read your book before the interview.

If you are new to TV interviews, talk to the interviewer, not to the camera. The time allotted for an interview passes quickly, try to cover the main points even if the interviewer is taking the interview in another direction. Keep and review copies of these interviews. TV and radio stations may give you a recording of the interview.

Bookmarks and business cards are worthwhile take-aways. If (when) you have several books include pictures of their covers and ordering information on your bookmarks.

Creating **marketing collateral** (business cards, bookmarks, flyers) isn't difficult, and you can create varieties for specific purposes. Don't want to do this yourself? Contact a local high school, community college, or college, and ask whether they can provide an intern to get experience in creating collateral. The intern may do it for free (as long as you give them an evaluation of their work), or they may charge a modest fee. I like to use local printers for these items, but if you want large quantities, you might consider online providers. vistaprint (www.vistaprint.com/) and moo (www.moo.com/).

Objections

Objections merit special consideration. "Objections" is an unfortunate word for the situation of a potential customer/client questioning a product or service. I prefer using "feedback" or "questions". Addressing objections is part of marketing, and objections can appear anywhere in a project. Hearing and addressing objections is far better than the customer just walking away. "I don't know." "It's too expensive." "I had trouble writing in school, so I gave up trying." "I have other priorities." "I don't have time." "I'm not interested." "I don't see how your book fits my needs." And others.

Objections are invitations for more information. Interpret objections as questions or a "Tell me more" prompt. Marketing is educating, listening, asking "why?", helping your prospect achieve their goals.

To anticipate objections, create your own FAQs (FAQ = Frequently Asked Question). You make up the questions, then you answer the questions. This prepares you for interacting with your audience. As you encounter objections, write them down, address them, and add them to your FAQ list.

Other Publishing Approaches

Reading this section is optional if you plan to use KDP as your POD service.

If you are unsure of using KDP, I suggest you use the KDP model as a benchmark when exploring any self-publishing service.

Why not get an **agent or a traditional publisher**? If you can define your market, and your market meshes with the market(s) agents or traditional publishers target, then you MAY be successful using that strategy.

"MAY be successful"? Agents and publishers are VERY SELECTIVE. They get bombarded with hundreds of candidate manuscripts every year, and they may limit themselves to producing only six (for example) titles per year. The new-book acceptance rate may be very low. The traditional publisher route sounds appealing, but the amount of time that passes between your submission (if it's accepted) and your book appearing on the market may be a year or longer. And it may even take months to learn whether your submission has been accepted or not.

Can you wait that long? There are a number of reasons why the answer may be "No". You are impatient to get your book out since you have invested so much of your time on it. The topic is timely. You want to be first or early into the market. Your audience is ready. You wonder whether you will have enough life left to get your book published (this is a sad reason, but you just never know).

You may think *But, I'm different* or *But my book is different*. Maybe so, but getting your work into the "slush pile", getting it read (rather than scanned) can be an uphill battle. If you do get a traditional publisher deal your royalties per book may be lower than with self-publishing. You will still do a lot of marketing, and any advance your might get is an advance against royalties, so you receive no royalties until the advance amount is covered..

Vanity Presses – you pay them for a quantity of your books, they ship them to you as inventory for you to sell, gift, or store. They MAY list your book online (for an extra fee).

Local printers – similar to Vanity Presses, but with a localized audience/market.

There are 25 or more SPSs offering a variety of packages. Google 'print on demand' for a list. Their services may be packaged or ala carte. Their fees range from the $800's up into five figures. Not all SPSs offer the same services, not all SPSs price their offerings similarly. Some charge extra ($$) for a second printed proof copy. Keep in mind that these services earn their profit based on the services they offer and charge for, not on the success of your book. They usually make your book available online. They may offer a conversion service to make your book into an eBook (for an extra fee). They may help with marketing, but this help may be limited to making marketing collateral.

If you are considering any SPS, I suggest you *Google <SPSname> complaints*. Every service has complaints; it's important that you be aware of them, although many complaints are weak.

Fulfillment

Fulfillment is the step that fills orders, packaging your book and shipping it to your customers. It sounds simple, and it is. If you have to ship more than a few books, this process can get to be tedious. What if you get 100 orders for your book? Wouldn't you rather be writing?

Online booksellers handle fulfillment, handle sales tax collection, and provide annual (at least) sales reports for income tax purposes. Some local printers may handle fulfillment. Some companies specialize in fulfillment.

Fulfillment costs money for warehousing, packaging, and shipping.

Let the SPS or the POD handle it. Spend your time writing and selling.

Hybrid

Hybrid is a popular (and somewhat vague) adjective in SPS marketing: hybrid author, hybrid publisher, hybrid contract. A **hybrid author** publishes books in both traditional and self-publisher modes. The advantage of this is that a traditional publisher may spot a self-published book and seek to incorporate it, or a derivative of it into their offerings. A **hybrid publisher** provides an eBook conversion process from a print manuscript. This can be useful for the author.

In the **hybrid contract** (SPSs may use other names) the publisher offers to charge you a "fraction" of their normal charge, and collect the remainder from royalties. Almost feels like an advance. However, the publisher has already made its money, so they are not really investing in you or your book.

Middleman

Some SPSs are marketing fronts for other companies that do the real SPS work. I consider the fronts to be "middlemen" collecting a front-end fee, but not doing the work. I'm not against using the middleman model, but it's important to be aware. They may not offer customer service directly, but they relay requests and responses. If you are getting serious about any specific SPS, Google its name. The listing may show an item "Parent Company". This could reflect a middleman arrangement.

A way to look at this is that there is one SPS service that does the publishing-related work through a number of "outlets". These outlets may *seem* to be competitors, may offer different services, or the same services under different names, and may charge different fees for their services. This is really a marketing strategy.

"They Want MY Book"

I've heard anecdotes of SPSs being enthusiastic about an author's book. One author told me "They want **MY** book!" I suggest that statement really says "They want **ANY** book". SPSs make their money on their services, paid for by the authors.

Profitability

Profitability depends on revenues (royalties for online sales, margin for self-sell) and costs.

Royalties are a function of printing cost and list price. Various SPSs have their own royalty calculation formulas. Two of these methods are:

> Percent of sell price (which could be discounted from list).

Percent of net (sell price – cost).

If you are considering an SPS other than KDP, be certain you understand their royalty calculation rules.

The margin for self-sell is easy to determine: subtract the costs per book sold from the sell price of the book. The trick here is knowing the author-sell cost of the book. Be certain you understand their cost calculation rules.

Ask the SPS representative questions to be sure you understand their offerings and their process. Make sure you understand the net VALUE of their offerings versus their costs to you before you sign up.

SPS Contract

Ask the SPS representative for a copy of the contract before you sign anything and before you give them any money. Review the contract in detail and make sure you understand the costs you may incur.

Copyright

Copyright is the legal mechanism to protect your Intellectual Property interests in your creative work. (uspto.gov/copyright)

The **copyright** notice (usually on the back of the title page) identifies you as the author, and the holder of copyright for the work. Basically, if you created it, the copyright is yours, even if you didn't include the © notice. If you acquired content (text or images) from someone else, you need to get written permission for use. Get the agreement in writing.

"But I trust . . ." Get the agreement in writing. The written agreement protects both parties.

Checkout the copyright page for this booklet. To strengthen copyright protection, register your book with the Library of Congress (LoC). This is not complicated; the LoC provides an online how-to description and an interactive process. If you detect plagiarism of your work, the registered copyright is vital to move forward, the better your chance of prevailing. Note that "Fair Use" allows limited use of copyrighted material without specific permission.

"Copyright" is a noun, not a verb.

There's a notion that mailing a copy of your work to yourself and not opening the package until you need to prove that you wrote it provides ample evidence of copyright ownership. It's sometimes called the poor man's copyright. It's not. It has no legal standing.

Use Rights

Use rights enable you to allow others to use your material subject to certain restrictions or allow you to use the materials of others. This can be a way to earn more money from your book. Use rights must be documented in writing, including fees, time frames, and what happens at the end of the granting of the rights. This documentation protects all parties involved. Here are typical use rights:

FNASR = First North America Serial Rights: a print periodical (newspaper, magazine) reproduce your work in North America (US and Canada). This does not permit inclusion in an anthology.

FR = First Rights, similar to FNASR without the geographic limitation.

OTR = One Time Rights, a non-exclusive right to use the material one time.

SR = Second Rights, aka Reprint Rights, states that the material has already been published.

ER = Electronic Rights, may be refined by type of electronic media (internet, DVD, CD, website/blog. Electronic rights should be thoroughly understood and documented.

AR = All Rights, no limitations, but you cannot sell the material again, possibly not even revisions or rewrites of the material. You do retain the right to claim ownership. If you sell All Rights you cannot even use the material on your own website/blog.

Work for Hire = the copyright is owned by the person who created the work, unless the artist sells the copyright or the person was hired to create the work.

Even if you have transferred rights you may be able to regain them - ask the publisher; they may no longer have any interest in the article. If they do return the rights to you, get the return agreement in writing.

There are two other rights options: **Creative Commons** and **Copyleft**. Using these, the author allows others to use the material, usually with attribution. Each of these includes a number of options. For more information, see *http://us.creativecommons.org/* or *http://en.wikipedia.org/wiki/Copyleft*.

Fair Use allows an author to quote a limited a portion of material without seeking formal permission. The quoting must be for educational or explanatory purposes. If in doubt, seek permission from the author to use it, or paraphrase it.

Copyright is an important area to understand. Contact an Intellectual Property Attorney and/or check out (uspto.gov/copyright) for more information.

Financial

This is a broad-brush overview of the financial aspects of the book business. More information is available online and from a business or tax accountant.

If your book will be a gift or if it will be embedded in an offering such as a workshop, you are most concerned about cost, since you do not expect to derive any direct revenue.

If you plan to sell your book, then you want to "break-even". Break-even is the point at which sales of your books cover the costs of your books. Sound simple, but maybe not.

There are two classes of expenses to consider: fixed costs and variable costs.

Variable costs are related to the "cost per book sold". Online sales are easy to deal with, the seller handles the "paperwork" and the fee administration. For self-sell, you handle the paperwork and the fee administration. This includes tracking costs for proof and draft copies, for purchase and receipt of inventory, and revenues for sale of inventory including shipping and tax. The costs vary based on the sales volume.

Fixed costs are related to your overall book project and include equipment purchase/lease, supplies, marketing collateral. Editing services, research material, subscriptions, office/space rental.

Travel (research, book signings), refreshments at book signings, can be accounted for as either variable cost or fixed cost.

A spreadsheet is viable tool to track revenues and costs. Computer apps are available to help with the recordkeeping and report generation. For each item, record date, amount, revenue (as positive), cost (as negative), venue/customer, provider, and any other information you may need at the end of the year for business performance analysis and for tax reporting.

You have the option to amortize (distribute) some of the fixed costs over the number of books that you estimate you will sell.

There's a myth that if you report your income for income tax purposes you need not collect/remit the sales tax. That's not the way it works. In New York State, you can apply for a NYS Certificate of Authority to collect NYS Sales tax. The certificate is free, and you will be required to remit your sales tax collected periodically throughout the year. Other localities may have their own sales tax requirements.

About the Author

The **About the Author** chapter in your book provides a vehicle to educate your customer with your background, your credentials. Items you might include are your education, your experience, your interests, your hobbies, your memberships, your other books. I suggest you write this chapter in the third person.

Here's my About the Author:

Mike Miller designs books. What's that mean? Author(s) provide content (text and images) and Mike puts the book together based on discussions to determine the characteristics of the finished product. Mike's book design process includes copyediting and cover creation.

In addition to designing books, Mike conducts Self-Publishing sessions and in-depth workshops.

Many of the 40-plus books Mike has designed for some 20 authors are available on Amazon.com in print format, most in Kindle format also.

Mike is a retired Computer Software Design Engineer and Director. And he does a few other things: stereography, photography, writing, painting, and quilting.

It's Your Book, Create It, Publish It, Market It – A Guide to Self-Publishing

What If – An Exploration into the Mind

Wordfinderz – difficult word search puzzles

Acrostic Poetry- and some prose

Concise Guide to Self-Publishing (you're reading it right now)

Acknowledgements

My writing and this book have been influenced by many people, far more than I can list, and more than I recall. I hereby thank them all. Suffice it to say that those who have read my earlier self-publishing guide *It's You Book – Create It, Publish It, Market It* have provided a number of suggestions and comments that have influenced the content of this book.

I thank the members of the Lewiston Writers' Group, the Lockport Write Touch Writers' Group, and the Northside Writers, all western New You writing groups.

I thank the many authors who have engaged me to help them with their self-publishing projects. Our interaction has helped me to continually be aware of the interested and preferences for their book ambitions, and for the many approaches they have shown in their pursuing and achieving their writing and book goals.

Your Project Profile

Tasks - ...do yourself? ...need to learn more? ...seek help form others?	Your self	Learn more	Others who?
Determining your motivation Why are you writing your book?			
Identifying your team			
Planning your project When to hit the market?			
Identifying your audience			
Assessing the Quality of your book (ongoing)			
Doing market research			
Doing content research			

Acquiring your content
   Writing
   Images			

Critiquing your manuscript/proof			
Reviewing, revising, refining			
Designing the Layout			
Designing the Cover (front, back, spine)			
Evaluating self-publishing services If you plan to not use KDP			

Managing your manuscript:
   Account setup
   Submission
   Proof review
   Metadata setup
   Author self-sell copies			

Registering copyright			

Promoting and selling your book
   Where
   Handling objections
   Social media			

Interviewing for TV and Radio